W9-AJP-294

EAST NORTHPORT, NEW YORK

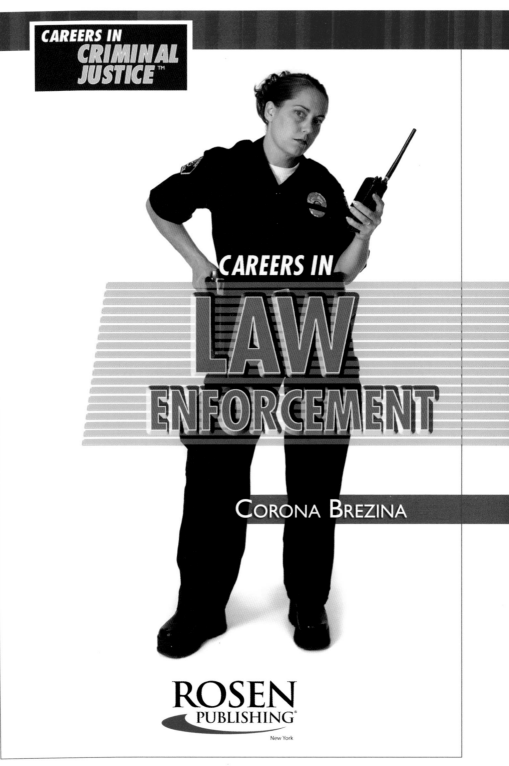

CAREERS IN
CRIMINAL
JUSTICE™

CAREERS IN

LAW
ENFORCEMENT

CORONA BREZINA

ROSEN
PUBLISHING®

New York

Published in 2010 by The Rosen Publishing Group, Inc.
29 East 21st Street, New York, NY 10010

Copyright © 2010 by The Rosen Publishing Group, Inc.

First Edition

All rights reserved. No part of this book may be reproduced in any form without permission in writing from the publisher, except by a reviewer.

**Library of Congress Cataloging-in-Publication Data**

Brezina, Corona.
Careers in law enforcement / Corona Brezina.—1st ed.
    p. cm.—(Careers in criminal justice)
Includes bibliographical references and index.
ISBN-13: 978-1-4358-5264-8 (library binding)
1. Law enforcement—Vocational guidance—United States.
2. Police—Vocational guidance—United States. 3. Job
hunting—United States. I. Title.
HV8143.B75 2010
363.2023'73—dc22

                                                    2008040856

*Manufactured in China*

# CONTENTS

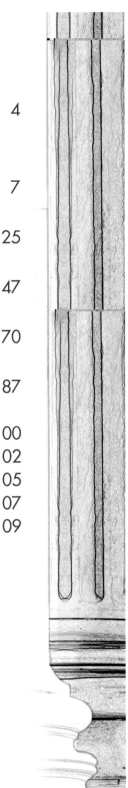

# INTRODUCTION

Criminal justice is an exciting field with a broad range of possible career paths for young people interested in a challenging and rewarding line of work. The criminal justice system is made up of the organizations and agencies responsible for preventing and punishing crime. Law enforcement organizations are charged with investigating crimes and arresting suspects. Accused criminals are tried in the court system and, if convicted, given a sentence. They then pass on to the corrections component of the criminal justice system, which includes prisons, jails, and programs such as probation and parole.

For most citizens, law enforcement officers represent the authority of the criminal justice system in their daily lives. Local officers patrol neighborhoods, investigate crimes, and direct traffic. State officers patrol state highways and enforce state laws. Further removed from everyday activities, federal agents enforce federal law for numerous agencies within different departments of the government.

Sgt. Matthew Brannock of the Virginia State Police was one of the first officers on the scene following the April 16, 2007, Virginia Tech massacre committed by Seung-Hui Cho.

On every level—and in the private sector—law enforcement offers a range of opportunities. A new recruit may aim for a promotion, a position with another agency, or the acquisition of specialized skills. Departments require specialists in a variety of areas, ranging from computer crime experts to canine handlers. In addition, an individual with a strong background in law enforcement can likely find a job in any part of the country, since police officers are needed in large cities as well as the most isolated rural areas.

Law enforcement work sometimes requires that an officer handle emergency or crisis situations, but it also consists of routine duties such as patrolling an area or writing reports. A day on the job for a law enforcement officer might involve chasing down a notorious criminal, consulting with forensic experts about evidence from a crime scene, or testifying for a court case. Whether participating in a hostage standoff or a community meeting, a law enforcement officer has the unique satisfaction at the end of the day of knowing that he or she personally played a part in ensuring that justice was upheld.

# PREPARING FOR A CAREER IN LAW ENFORCEMENT

A law enforcement career can be exciting, varied, fascinating, and challenging. At the same time, it can be demanding, dangerous, tedious, and stressful. Above all, though, law enforcement is a rewarding career. Law enforcement officers are responsible for apprehending criminals and keeping the public safe and secure. They know that their work makes the peace and order of daily life possible.

The field of law enforcement offers many possible career paths. There are multitudes of positions in local police departments, state police departments, and federal agencies. Within these departments, officers specialize in areas such as computer crime, the canine corps, arson investigation, SWAT team operations, and much more. There are also law enforcement career options in the private sector. Private investigators, security guards, and forensic professionals do their part to maintain order and help carry out justice.

Law enforcement is not for everyone. An officer must possess a high degree of training as well as exceptional skills and personal qualities. If a candidate's main interest in the job lies in the chance to carry a gun and order people around, then that person is not a good fit for the job. If, on the other hand, the candidate wants to work to keep communities safe, uphold the law, and play a part in bringing criminals to justice, then he or she could prove to be an asset to the department.

## WHAT IT TAKES

When an applicant for a law enforcement job walks into a group interview, the interviewers will already be familiar with his or her background based on a résumé and other application materials. In addition to evaluating firsthand the candidate's experience and suitability, the interviewers will be looking for certain skills and personal qualities.

A law enforcement officer must have superior leadership abilities. An officer may be required to enter a tense or dangerous situation and immediately take control. During routine duties, an officer may interview witnesses, interact with members of the community, or deal with panicked victims of a crime. Good leadership skills are essential to inspiring confidence and providing others with direction and guidance.

New York City police officers Carlos Suarez (*left*) and Ryan Jackson (*top right*) talk to teens at a recruiting event. The NYPD is the largest and most diverse force in the country.

An officer must also exhibit good judgment, whether in a split-second decision or in a drawn-out situation that requires problem-solving skills. In some circumstances, making the right judgment call can save lives or lead to a criminal being captured.

The modern law enforcement officer must have excellent communication and interpersonal skills. In the past, police officers had a reputation for being tough, hard, and aggressive. Today, law enforcement officers work to build and sustain relationships with the community and the public. Officers must be able to communicate effectively in circumstances that might call for sensitivity to cultural differences, that might involve hostile individuals, or that might require clear and concise information due to a crisis situation. They should be prepared to work with other officers in teams or formal task forces. Written communication skills, too, are critical to producing effective reports.

The ethical expectations of a law enforcement officer are stated in the International Association of Chiefs of Police (IACP) Code of Conduct. The code outlines the primary responsibilities of a police officer and describes the appropriate attitude an officer should have during the performance of duties. Officers should use discretion in enforcing the law—issuing a warning, rather than taking legal action under some circumstances, for example. An officer should not use unnecessary force. Officers should have integrity—they should act fairly and reject the temptations of bribery and corruption. They should cooperate fully with colleagues from other law enforcement agencies. Throughout their careers, officers should aim to increase their knowledge and improve their professional performance. An officer should lead a law-abiding private life.

A law enforcement officer must accept that there are dangers associated with the job. Police officers are required to deal with high-risk situations that could potentially involve a confrontation with an armed and desperate suspect. According to P. J. Ortmeier's *Introduction to Law Enforcement and Criminal Justice*, officers are most likely to be injured or killed while making an arrest, interrupting a robbery or burglary, intervening in a domestic dispute, or conducting a vehicle stop. Even some federal positions that sound like "safe" jobs require that agents be trained in handling firearms and making arrests. Don't forget that notorious Chicago crime boss Al Capone was nabbed by Internal Revenue Service (IRS) agents!

In addition to the risks of law enforcement work, there are other considerations that might make some job hunters think twice about whether they are a good match for the work. A career in law enforcement can take a toll on an officer's

personal life. The job requires long hours, sometimes including night and weekend work, and police work can be incredibly stressful. Officers often find it difficult to leave their on-duty mentality behind them when their shift is over. In some cases, this can result in family conflicts, substance abuse, and even suicide. Some law enforcement organizations offer counseling and other resources to officers and their families.

Although routine, traffic stops must be viewed as potentially dangerous situations and conducted with caution and attention to detail.

## GETTING THE JOB

The application and pre-employment screening for job openings in law enforcement is an intensive process. Applicants are put through numerous examinations, tests, and interviews. Before hiring candidates, law enforcement recruiters run background checks on them. They weigh factors such as financial and criminal records—individuals with a

# Police Academy 101: The Miranda Warning

**Before** a crime suspect in custody is questioned, police are required to advise the suspect of these five constitutional rights:

- You have the right to remain silent.
- Anything you say can and will be used against you in a court of law.
- You have the right to an attorney.
- If you cannot afford an attorney, one will be appointed to represent you if you wish.
- You can decide at any time to stop answering questions if you wish.

This advisory, known as the Miranda warning, dates from the landmark 1966 case of *Miranda v. Arizona*. Ernesto Miranda was tried and convicted for the 1963 kidnapping and rape of a young woman. He appealed his case to the Supreme Court on the basis that before his confession, police had not informed him of these rights, which are derived from the Fifth and Sixth Amendments of the U.S. Constitution. The Supreme Court ruled in his favor. (Later, Miranda was convicted of the crime even without admission of his confession in court.)

It is not necessary for police to "Mirandize" every witness they question. But for a suspect in custody, neglecting to recite the Miranda warning could make the suspect's statement inadmissible in court.

past felony conviction, domestic violence conviction, or recent drug use cannot become law enforcement officers.

Any young person with aspirations of becoming a law enforcement officer should start out by establishing a reputation as a good citizen and avoiding pitfalls that might blemish a background check. Obey the law. Minor offenses such as one or two parking or traffic tickets won't disqualify a candidate, but employers might frown upon a pattern of irresponsible driving, especially if citations are unpaid. Manage personal finances wisely, since an unsound financial history may indicate a lack of responsibility in a candidate.

One sure way for a job seeker to improve employment prospects is to continue his or her education. A college education supplies the candidate with specialized skills and knowledge, as well as critical thinking and communication skills. College students also gain experience in interacting with people from diverse backgrounds. A two-year or four-year degree can give an applicant an edge in the hiring process. Many federal agencies require that applicants for some positions hold a bachelor's degree.

Recruiters generally pay close attention to an applicant's employment history, but young people and recent graduates just starting out do not have an extensive work history. When this is the case, applicants should emphasize their related education and experiences that make them stand out from the rest of the candidates. An applicant may have done volunteer work in the community, perhaps tutoring children or participating in a leadership program run by the police department. Students can complete internships at police departments, at various federal or state agencies, in the court system, or with a variety of other organizations related to law enforcement.

Any job applicant is anxious to know the salary and benefits that come with the position. Pay for law enforcement officers varies greatly, depending on factors such as an individual's experience and education, and whether they live in a metropolitan or rural area. Law enforcement job listings in the newspaper and online should give applicants an idea of typical earnings for their geographical region and level of experience. In addition, national statistics on wages for a variety of career areas are listed in the U.S. Bureau of Labor Statistics' *Occupational Employment Statistics*, which can be accessed online at http://www.bls.gov/oes.

## AT THE ACADEMY

Before a new law enforcement officer begins work, he or she must complete training at a police academy. This training will equip the officer with

Recruits complete hundreds of hours of training and instruction, such as firearms practice, over a period of several months.

the knowledge, skills, and abilities necessary to perform the job. The training period generally lasts from two to six months.

Police academy is a rigorous and intensive course that combines classroom instruction with practical training. A recruit learns the laws that he or she will have to enforce, the protocol for writing reports, and investigative techniques. He or she spends time on the firing range, learning about weapons, and in the gym, learning self-defense, arrest techniques, and the appropriate use of force. The hours spent on vehicular operation are particularly valuable—more officers are killed in car accidents than are killed by criminals.

Here is a sample course curriculum for basic training, required by the California Commission on Peace Officer Standards and Training:

- Leadership, Professionalism, and Ethics – 8 hours
- Criminal Justice System – 2 hours
- Policing in the Community – 18 hours
- Victimology/Crisis Intervention – 6 hours
- Introduction to Criminal Law – 4 hours
- Property Crimes – 6 hours
- Crimes Against Persons/Death Investigation – 6 hours
- General Criminal Statutes – 2 hours

*(continued)*

# Tips for a Great Law Enforcement Résumé

**Your** résumé serves as a way for you to introduce yourself to prospective employers when applying for a job. A well-constructed résumé provides relevant information that demonstrates why you are a good candidate for the position. Here are a few tips:

Start by highlighting your strengths. If you have an impressive work record, then list that first. If you're a recent graduate but you've done a lot of community service or volunteer work, then start there.

Tailor your résumé to the prospective position. You want to emphasize different skills and qualifications for a local police department job than for a federal position.

Spell out your qualifications clearly. Instead of giving a description of a former job or activity, list the skills and experience you gained that are relevant to the position you're applying for.

Have your résumé double-checked. Friends or family members who know you well might be able to suggest points to add. An adviser at your school's career center or a professional law enforcement officer might also offer advice on how to impress prospective employers.

- Crimes Against Children – 4 hours
- Sex Crimes – 4 hours
- Juvenile Law and Procedure – 3 hours
- Controlled Substances – 12 hours
- ABC (alcoholic beverage) Law – 2 hours
- Laws of Arrest – 12 hours
- Search and Seizure – 12 hours
- Presentation of Evidence – 6 hours
- Investigative Report Writing – 52 hours
- Vehicle Operations – 24 hours
- Use of Force – 12 hours
- Patrol Techniques – 12 hours
- Vehicle Pullovers – 14 hours
- Crimes in Progress – 20 hours
- Handling Disputes/Crowd Control – 8 hours
- Domestic Violence – 10 hours
- Unusual Occurrences – 4 hours
- Missing Persons – 4 hours
- Traffic Enforcement – 16 hours
- Traffic Collision Investigations – 12 hours
- Crime Scenes, Evidence, and Forensics – 12 hours
- Custody – 2 hours
- Lifetime Fitness – 44 hours
- Arrest Methods/Defensive Tactics – 60 hours

- First Aid and CPR – 21 hours
- Firearms/Chemical Agents – 72 hours
- Information Systems – 2 hours
- People with Disabilities – 6 hours
- Gang Awareness – 2 hours
- Crimes Against the Justice System – 4 hours
- Weapons Violations – 4 hours
- Hazardous Materials Awareness – 4 hours
- Cultural Diversity/Discrimination – 16 hours
- Emergency Management – 16 hours

California, for example, requires 560 class hours, as well as 104 hours of testing, for a total of 664 hours, for its peace officers, which are local police officers as well as state police, sheriff's deputies, and other public safety personnel.

Small police departments generally send their trainees to regional or state academies. Large police departments operate their own academies. Officers in the New York City Police Department, for example, are trained in the NYPD Academy run by the NYPD Training Bureau. State-level police officers are trained at the state academy.

Many federal law enforcement agents are trained at the Federal Law Enforcement Training Center (FLETC). Federal agents receive basic training

in the Criminal Investigator Training Program, the Land Management Training Program, or the Mixed Basic Police Training Program. As with any police academy, this includes both classroom time and hands-on training. The U.S. Secret Service, the U.S. Marshals Service, Customs and Border Protection, and dozens of other agencies train their employees at FLETC. In addition, local and state departments can send their officers to FLETC for specialized training. FLETC also offers three

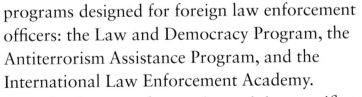

Instructor John Florence stands by as two Park Service Rangers practice arrest techniques at the Federal Law Enforcement Training Center (FLETC) in Georgia.

programs designed for foreign law enforcement officers: the Law and Democracy Program, the Antiterrorism Assistance Program, and the International Law Enforcement Academy.

Federal agents also receive training specific to their agency, sometimes through FLETC and sometimes at their agency's facilities. Border patrol agents, for example, learn immigration law and study Spanish. IRS agents are trained in tax laws and recovering computer evidence. ATF agents learn about arson investigation and bomb scene investigation. Training programs for federal agents generally run for a minimum of sixteen weeks.

The most famous law enforcement training program in the country is probably the FBI Academy in Quantico, Virginia. It is academically rigorous. Throughout the course, Federal Bureau of Investigation (FBI) trainees must achieve 85 percent on exams in legal issues, behavioral science, interviewing, ethics, investigative techniques, interrogation, and forensic science. Trainees must maintain the highest levels of physical fitness, and they are penalized if they do not pass fitness tests. They must master self-defense techniques, handling weapons, and arrest techniques. There is also a Practical Exercises and Evaluation portion. Some of the hours in this segment are spent in a small "town" called Hogan's Alley, where role players act the part of criminals and witnesses during simulated FBI operations.

# CAREERS AT THE LOCAL AND STATE LEVELS

For most people, their local police force is the public face of law enforcement in the United States. Local police officers are generally the first responders to any emergency. They direct traffic, patrol neighborhoods, and enforce the laws within their city limits. Behind the scenes, they run investigations of crimes, manage the administrative details of their caseload, and testify in court.

A local department can range in size from a one-man municipal force serving a small town to a metropolitan police force made up of thousands of officers. Regardless of the size of their department, most police officers are responsible for a wide range of duties. Larger departments, however, often offer greater opportunity for advancement. Police departments in large cities employ specialists in different areas and detectives who serve in units devoted to specific offenses, such as narcotics, arson, or vice.

# JOINING A LOCAL POLICE DEPARTMENT

Hiring procedures vary from one local department to the next, as do entrance requirements for prospective employees. Some departments have a minimum age of twenty-one and a maximum age of thirty-five or forty. In some areas, recent high school graduates with a passion for law enforcement may familiarize themselves with the field by enrolling in a cadet program. They can acquire valuable practical experience serving as a community service officer (CSO) or in a similar capacity until they reach the minimum age to apply for a job as an officer.

As with all law enforcement jobs, those who want to become local police officers must undergo rigorous screening. This generally includes a written test, interviews, a medical examination, psychological testing, a polygraph examination, and a background check that takes character as well as legal records into account. Some departments may give categorical preference to some groups in hiring. Examples include women, members of a minority group, veterans, or the relatives of fallen police officers. Some departments may require that job seekers live in the city, county, or state in which they are applying.

Local police officers must have a high school diploma or a General Educational Development

(GED) credential, and many departments require higher levels of education. Some require a certain number of college credits, an associate's degree, or less commonly, a four-year degree. Even when departments do not require higher education, some college coursework—especially in the field of criminal justice—will likely give a job applicant an edge.

Some departments require that applicants successfully complete police academy training in advance of applying for the job. In general, though, newly hired officers attend police academy as part of their probation period, which generally lasts a minimum of six months. New recruits also undergo on-the-job-training (OTJ) or field training during their probation period in order to gain practical experience.

Most police departments have a formal procedure for promotion to higher ranks. Officers are generally required to serve for five years before being considered for promotion to lieutenant, then two more years before being considered for captain. The chief of police is the highest-level officer in a municipal police department. Factors weighed in selecting finalists include written exams, seniority, performance evaluations, and an interview. A higher rank may require higher levels of education, and some departments pay some or all of the tuition for an officer to obtain a degree in criminal justice or other relevant fields.

## PATROL OFFICER

Most recruits start out by patrolling an assigned beat. They are often required to work "in the field" as patrol officers for two years before being reassigned or promoted within the patrol division. Patrol officers typically work forty-hour weeks that may include night shifts, since police departments must maintain twenty-four-hour service.

Newly sworn in police officers toss their gloves in the air during a New York Police Department Police Academy graduation ceremony.

The patrol division is frequently described as the backbone of the police department. It is the largest operating unit in most police departments, whether on a municipal, metropolitan, sheriff, or state level. Patrol officers also have the most direct contact with the community—they represent the arm of the law in the everyday lives of citizens.

Patrol officers are assigned to a specific district. They are expected to become intimately familiar with the boundaries, layout, landmarks, traffic patterns, community leaders, and other features of their beat. Officers often work with a partner in marked police cars when they are on vehicular patrol. They may patrol on bicycles, on horseback, or on motorcycle. In some areas, such as congested downtown locations, officers may patrol on foot. Some places may require air patrol or marine patrol.

When on duty, patrol officers are expected to prevent crime, apprehend criminals, and preserve the peace. They respond to dispatches from police headquarters and direct requests for help from the public. These may cover a huge range of situations. Patrol officers respond to reports of possible crimes as well as to circumstances such as accidents, emergencies, disturbances of the peace, reports of missing persons, and threats to public safety. Depending on the situation, they may have to make an arrest, issue a citation, mount a preliminary investigation, or redirect a complaint to a different authority. Patrol officers enforce parking and traffic regulations and respond to vehicular accidents. When necessary, they administer first aid. They provide crowd control at public events. They also address the day-to-day concerns of the public and support crime prevention efforts in the community.

Mounted patrols are useful in areas that are inconvenient or inaccessible for foot or vehicle patrols, such as in downtown Austin, Texas.

# William J. Bratton

**William J. Bratton,** former New York City police commissioner, has established an international reputation for his crime-fighting initiatives. During his time at the NYPD, Bratton oversaw the development of the CompStat system of mapping crimes. It organized data on crime and arrests, enabling the department to deploy officers to specific high-crime areas, prepared with up-to-date information and reliable intelligence. Under Bratton's leadership, crime rates dropped dramatically and morale improved among the NYPD.

A native of Boston, Bratton attended the University of Massachusetts, where he earned a bachelor of science degree in law enforcement. He also graduated from the FBI National Executive Institute and completed a fellowship at the John F. Kennedy School of Government at Harvard University. He began his career as an officer with the Boston Police Department.

In 2002, Bratton was appointed chief of the Los Angeles Police Department. He began his second term in 2007, becoming the first police chief reappointed to the post since 1992.

# TRAFFIC OFFICER

Traffic officers focus on regulating the flow of traffic and enforcing traffic laws. The traffic officer has an important, and sometimes dangerous, job. A typical day may involve rerouting traffic and testifying in court, but it could also include a high-speed chase of a desperate suspect, dealing with "road rage" from a frustrated driver, or stopping someone suspected of DUI (driving under the influence).

In a sense, traffic officers are specialized patrol officers. Their primary goal is to guarantee that traffic is able to move as safely and efficiently as possible. They generally drive a marked police car and work alone. Under some circumstances—in congested areas, near accident sites, or in school zones—they will direct traffic on foot.

Traffic officers issue citations for both parking violations and moving violations such as speeding, making illegal turns, aggressive driving, or failing to yield. Some departments have a separate unit specializing in parking violations. Traffic officers also issue equipment violations, such as for shattered windshields or broken lights, and document violations, such as for out-of-date plates or no proof of insurance. Traffic officers play an important role in locating stolen or wanted vehicles, which may be identified during a routine

Police and other emergency responders in Amsterdam, New York, work to rescue a driver and passenger trapped in a car.

traffic stop. They also see to the removal of abandoned vehicles and report malfunctioning stoplights and other potential safety hazards.

One of the traffic officer's most important duties is responding to the scene of a collision. The traffic officer manages the scene, investigates the cause, and restores the flow of traffic as quickly as possible. The officer's first priority is tending to the injured. Later, information from his or her report may be used to improve safety measures at the site of the accident.

## DETECTIVE

Detectives investigate criminal cases, often taking over where the duties of patrol officers leave off. They dress in civilian clothes (they may receive a clothing allowance) and drive unmarked cars. Detectives usually work with a partner. A uniformed officer generally has to spend at least three years on the force before being promoted to the rank of detective. The job requires long hours and carries a huge responsibility, but it is a highly respected and coveted position.

Detectives are assigned a case and work on it until it is closed or dropped. They conduct follow-up interviews, investigate crime scenes, locate stolen property, coordinate with experts and other interested parties, and review evidence. In many cases, their primary goal is the identification and arrest of the offender. Like other members of the police force, detectives are responsible for considerable administrative work, such as filing reports and helping to prepare court cases.

Most detectives specialize in investigating a particular area of crime, such as homicide, sex crimes, narcotics, burglary, arson, forgery, fraud, auto theft, juvenile crimes, gang activity, hate crimes, computer forensics, or property crimes. Vice detectives investigate activities such as prostitution, gambling, and liquor law violations. White-collar detectives investigate cases such as corporate fraud, money laundering, and financial crimes. Detectives' duties evolve in response to changing trends in crime, such as an increase in certain drug-related activity or a rise in instances of identity theft.

## SPECIALIZED ASSIGNMENTS AND UNITS

Large police departments have units that specialize in a particular area of law enforcement. A specialized assignment will generally require additional education or training. Specialty units focus on specific types of crimes—see the above list of detective specialties. Specialized patrols are composed of their own units. A helicopter on air patrol might be utilized for routine traffic management or to track a

# The Texas Rangers

**The** Texas Rangers make up the oldest state law enforcement agency in the United States. Their early feats and traditions have made them legendary figures in the history and mythology of the Wild West.

The Texas Rangers organized unofficially in 1823, when Stephen F. Austin brought the first colonists to the state, which was then part of Mexico. The colonists formed a group to "range" the countryside and protect the citizens from bandits and hostile Native Americans. In 1835, a resolution formally constituted the Texas Rangers and established a hierarchy of ranks. When Texas became a republic a year later, companies of Texas Rangers were sent to protect the frontier, mainly against Native American attacks. In 1846, they aided the American army during the Mexican-American War, during which they were known as Los Diablos Tejanos—the Texas Devils—to the Mexicans. During the 1870s, the Texas Rangers chased down more than three thousand desperados, including the notorious outlaw John Wesley Hardin and Sam Bass, leader of a robber gang. In 1934, two former Texas Rangers led the posse that ended Bonnie Parker and Clyde Barrow's crime spree.

In 1935, the Texas Rangers were incorporated into the new Texas Department of Public Safety. Today, they are an elite group of 160 members, including 134 commissioned officers, charged with enforcing Texas state law as part of the Criminal Law Enforcement Division.

fugitive, while marine patrols are common in
seaports. Officers in the canine (K-9) corps are
paired with police dogs. K-9 teams may be called
in to track a missing person, sniff out bombs or
drugs, or help provide crowd control.

Some elite units specialize in resolving situations
such as a terrorist threat, riot, or standoff with an
armed suspect. In many police departments, the
specialists to call during a crisis are the Special
Weapons and Tactics (SWAT) team. Members of a

Specialized antigang units, such as this Miami task force, work to combat gang activity and related crimes, such as violence and drug trafficking.

SWAT team are trained in the use of specialized equipment—including assault weapons, tear gas grenades, high-tech surveillance gear, and body armor—and may employ paramilitary tactics during an operation. Officers must be in peak physical condition and pass a rigorous screening process before entering training, which can take two years. Large police departments have a SWAT unit with teams on call around the clock. In smaller police departments, SWAT team members perform regular police work in addition to their SWAT work and training.

# THE SHERIFF'S DEPARTMENT

In addition to local police departments, many states also have sheriff's departments that hold jurisdiction over counties. The sheriff is generally an elected official who is in charge of hiring deputy sheriffs that carry out the duties of the sheriff's department. The exact role of the sheriff's department varies from one state to another. (Some counties may have a county police department headed by a police chief.) Entrance requirements for positions in sheriff's departments and county police departments are similar to those of local police departments.

Like local police officers, deputy sheriffs patrol their area and investigate crimes, but they are also charged with duties related to the county court system. Deputy sheriffs may serve legal papers, such as subpoenas or court summons, and collect fees. They are also responsible for maintaining the jail, transporting inmates, and extraditing criminals from other jurisdictions. Within the courtroom, sheriff's deputies provide security and may serve as bailiffs.

Sheriff's departments serve larger areas than municipal and metropolitan police departments do.

In remote areas that are not served by local police departments, the sheriff's department sends out regular patrols and first responders to crimes. In larger cities, where metropolitan police largely fulfill these duties, the sheriff's department focuses on court and prison services.

## THE STATE POLICE

Every state in the United States, except for Hawaii, has a statewide police force—a highway patrol, a state police agency, or both. Most state law enforcement agencies are divisions of states' departments of public safety, though some units may be affiliated with their states' departments of justice. Organization and policies vary somewhat from one state to another.

State police enforce traffic laws on interstates and state highways. Although they have jurisdiction within cities and municipalities, they generally intervene in local law enforcement only in emergencies or other instances for which city or state officials request their services. They are also responsible for protecting the state capitol and other state government sites and providing security for the governor.

In some ways, it's easier for a job seeker to apply for a position with the state police—which has a single, centralized personnel department—than

Texas state troopers provide security at the Texas State Capitol, which houses the state legislature and the office of the governor.

local police, which may involve filling out a number of applications for departments with different hiring procedures. In general, job requirements for state police departments are similar to those of local departments in terms of age, education, background check, and selection process. New recruits go through a training course at the state police academy, similar to army recruit training.

State police officers can rise through the ranks because of experience and merit. Unlike local police departments, the state police system is generally based on a military system of organization—the lowest officer has a rank of private, and the superintendent bears the rank of colonel. States also employ civilians within the state police agencies for administrative work and specialized duties.

In addition, many state agencies other than the state police hire law enforcement personnel. Many state departments, from housing to public health to agriculture, need inspectors to investigate and enforce laws applicable to their areas of authority. A conservation officer working for a state's fish and wildlife service, for example, patrols the parks and other outdoor areas and enforces the pertinent laws. These might include state environmental regulations, laws against poaching, federal wildlife laws, and boating regulations.

## STATE POLICE CAREERS

Most new recruits begin by working as a state trooper or as a state highway patrol officer. They perform many of the same duties as local patrol officers, although over a far larger area. Unlike local patrol officers, state troopers generally work alone. For areas where there is no local, sheriff, or county department with jurisdiction, the state police functions as first responders and handles the day-to-day law enforcement duties.

Uniformed state troopers in marked police cars enforce traffic laws, issue citations, aid stranded drivers, and arrest suspected criminals. They monitor and report public safety hazards on the highways, such as weather-related conditions or wreckage left by accidents. State troopers also enforce weight regulations and other restrictions on commercial vehicles, such as semitrucks. Like local patrol officers, state troopers can be dispatched to the scene of accidents or other emergencies. They may also receive requests to help local police officers. State troopers play an important role in enforcing drug laws, since many drug dealers transport drugs across state lines. Some interstate highways are known as notorious drug routes. Like all law enforcement officers, state troopers spend time doing desk work and testifying in court cases.

An officer and a bomb-sniffing dog inspect trucks near a
checkpoint in New York City following the discovery of
an Al Qaeda plot to bomb financial institutions.

Most state police departments have specialized units, such as the Secretary of State Police or the K-9 unit. Criminal and civil cases within the state's jurisdiction are often handled by plainclothes investigators or by special agents within the State Bureau of Investigation, which is the state-level equivalent of the FBI. Investigators may specialize in certain types of crimes, such as narcotics, terrorism activity, or white-collar crime. Agents with a state's Bureau of Investigation may also provide aid to local police departments, especially in forensic investigations. They may consult in federal cases, too.

# 3

# CAREERS AT THE FEDERAL LEVEL

An enormous range of federal law enforcement job opportunities exists for applicants at various levels of education and experience. Careers in federal law enforcement can be appealing because of the good pay and benefits and the security of a government job. Most federal agencies list jobs with the Office of Personnel Management (OPM), and employment opportunities can be viewed online at http://www.usajobs.opm.gov. In addition, most agencies include a career section on their Web sites.

Federal law enforcement agencies generally require that an applicant be a U.S. citizen between the ages of twenty-one and thirty-seven. The individual job listing will specify the desired education and experience for that position. Most federal law enforcement agencies have a rigorous job application process that may include assorted exams (medical, psychological, aptitude, and more), interviews, a polygraph test, a drug screening, and a background check. Successful candidates complete a training program before starting the job. Many federal law enforcement agencies may require employees to relocate. Federal employees are classified by "grades" on the government's General Schedule. The salary for a particular position is determined by the grade and geographic location. Most federal law enforcement agents are required to retire at the age of fifty-seven.

Dozens of law enforcement agencies are associated with many different departments or organizations within the federal government. Many are affiliated with either the Department of Justice or the Department of Homeland Security. Following are the descriptions of some jobs in federal law enforcement agencies that have more than one thousand personnel with arrest and firearms authority.

## FBI SPECIAL AGENT

When people hear references to federal law enforcement, their thoughts often jump to the Federal Bureau of Investigation. The FBI is the arm of the Department of Justice that is charged with investigating more than two hundred types of federal crime. FBI investigations fall into seven general categories: counterterrorism, counter-intelligence (such as espionage), cybertechnology, public corruption, civil rights (such as hate crimes and police brutality cases), transnational/national crime (such as drug trafficking and human slavery), and white-collar crime. The FBI also performs background checks on applicants for a number of federal jobs.

The agency's headquarters are located in Washington, D.C. Fifty-six FBI field offices are located in cities across the United States and Puerto Rico. The FBI also operates forty-eight Legal Attaché (Legat) offices and six sub-offices across the world. Legats are affiliated with U.S. embassies in foreign countries, but they report to FBI headquarters. The FBI participates with other federal agencies in operating some joint programs, and it cooperates with various state, local, and international law enforcement agencies during some investigations.

FBI special agents have the broad powers to collect information and evidence related to their cases, but they do not authorize prosecutions and they have limited powers to arrest suspects. U.S. attorneys working for the Department of Justice determine whether or not to take action on a case. Therefore, agents often make regular reports to U.S. attorneys as they build their cases.

A case can range from a minor incident, such as disorderly conduct on board an airplane, to a major case involving a task force devoting years to an investigation on an international scale. A special agent may spend a day doing surveillance work,

conducting interviews, or reviewing recordings of wiretaps. In some cases, agents must go undercover or obtain information from informants. Like all law enforcement personnel, FBI agents devote a great deal of work to managing the administrative aspect of their cases and writing reports. The FBI is noted for its thoroughness with its files.

The FBI hiring process is lengthy, in-depth, and highly selective. According to *The FBI Career*

FBI new agent trainees train with shotguns at the FBI Academy in Quantico, Virginia. Training at the academy also includes a rigorous academic component.

*Guide* by Joseph W. Koletar, only about one out of every seventy applicants gets the job of FBI special agent. Applicants must be between the ages of twenty-three and thirty-six and have a bachelor's degree, preferably in an applicable field. They must also possess skills in categories necessary to the FBI, such as law, accounting, computer science, intelligence, engineering, physical sciences, or a foreign language. Factors such as past felonies or

# J. Edgar Hoover

**J. Edgar Hoover,** who served as director of the FBI from 1924 until his death in 1972, turned a weak and corrupt agency of about 650 people into one of the world's most recognized law enforcement organizations. Upon taking charge, Hoover raised the standards for agents and fired incompetent or corrupt employees. In 1924, he established the Identification Division, a huge collection of fingerprint records. The FBI training facility in Quantico, Virginia, was founded in 1928. In 1932, the FBI opened the Technical Laboratory, the forerunner of the FBI's forensic program. Hoover's overhaul established a reputation for the FBI as an efficient and elite organization. Hoover was also savvy at promoting his agency, publicizing its success in nabbing high-profile criminals during the 1930s.

Today, Hoover is considered a controversial historical figure, mainly for the authoritarian and even unconstitutional methods that he used later in his long career.

J. Edgar Hoover was so powerful that many presidents were afraid to replace him. Today, FBI directors are limited to a ten-year term.

some types of past drug activity automatically disqualify an applicant. The applicant must meet certain medical and fitness criteria.

Qualified applicants are invited to take a multiple-choice test that gauges their cognitive skills and situational judgment. Some applicants are nominated for the second phase of testing, which includes an interview with a panel of agents and a written essay. Those who pass phase two testing, as well as other procedures such as a polygraph test, drug testing, a background check, and a security interview, officially become new agent trainees (NATS). The next step is a sixteen-week training period at the FBI Academy in Quantico, Virginia.

Once they're on the job, recruits generally spend a two-year probation period under the supervision of a field training officer. They are often assigned to six to twelve months in the application squad, where they perform background checks on job applicants for federal positions. This stint, a good starting point for new agents, gives them a chance to improve their investigative skills and familiarize themselves with FBI procedures. Special agents should be willing to relocate whenever they are assigned or transferred to a different office.

Promotions are decided by career boards made up of senior FBI personnel. Most agents spend their entire careers as FBI special agents, often

FBI new agent trainees practice defensive tactics during training. Trainees accepted into the FBI should be in peak physical shape before starting the course.

developing specialized skills and taking on further responsibilities through their years of experience. Some agents apply for a promotion to the position of supervisory special agent (SSA), the head of a squad within a field office. The top position at a FBI field office is the special agent in charge (SAC). The SAC oversees all FBI activities carried out in the field office's area of operations, whether it's a city, a state, or a group of states.

Due to media and entertainment coverage, many people are interested in the position of FBI profiler, the agent who describes possible characteristics and motives of an unknown subject based on information and evidence. In reality, there is no such official job at the FBI. Profilers work for the National Center for the Analysis of Violent Crime (NCAVC) at Quantico, Virginia. Most applicants should have a background in behavioral science or forensic science, and they should have three years of work experience as an FBI special agent. Agents assigned to NCAVC complete five hundred hours of training.

## CBP OFFICER AND BORDER PATROL AGENT

Customs and Border Protection (CBP) officers and border patrol agents work for the U.S. Customs and Border Protection Agency, which is part of the Department of Homeland Security. The agency is charged with protecting lawful trade and travel across the land, sea, and air borders of the United States. CBP officers work at ports of entry to prevent people and goods from entering the country illegally. These might include illegal aliens, terrorists, drugs, or weapons. Personnel from the Department of Agriculture also perform inspections for the Customs and Border Protection Agency to ensure that livestock and plants imported into the country do not carry pests or diseases. Two key career opportunities within the agency are canine enforcement officer, who works with a dog trained to detect drugs, and special agent, who investigates cases of money laundering, drug and weapons trafficking, and other violations of federal trade laws.

Border patrol agents look out for illegal aliens and contraband on highways, in cities, in

An Immigration and Customs Enforcement (ICE) agent keeps watch during a raid in Boston, part of a national effort targeting illegal aliens with criminal records.

agricultural areas and, of course, on the border. Agents patrolling the border often work alone. They might follow the tracks of illegal aliens, conduct nighttime surveillance, monitor electronic sensors, or chase down suspects. New agents often start out the job manning a checkpoint station along the southwestern U.S. border shared with Mexico.

# U.S. IMMIGRATION AND CUSTOM ENFORCEMENT AGENTS

The U.S. Immigration and Custom Enforcement (ICE), which is part of the Department of Homeland Security, enforces laws pertaining to immigration, customs, and air security. It is organized into offices that specialize in a variety of enforcement activities. The Office of Investigations investigates cases related to human rights violations, trafficking in illegal arms, terrorism prevention, financial crimes, smuggling, cybercrime, and immigration crime or fraud. The Office of Detention and Removal detains high-risk illegal aliens, such as criminals, and removes or deports them according to the ruling of an immigration judge. The Office of Federal Protective Service oversees security measures for government facilities across the country. The Office of Intelligence supports the active branches of ICE and works with other federal agencies that are involved in intelligence.

## U.S. SECRET SERVICE SPECIAL AGENT

The U.S. Secret Service, which is an agency of the Department of Homeland Security, provides protection for public figures and conducts federal criminal investigations. Its "protectees" include the

Secret Service agents flank the motorcade as President George W. Bush rides in the 2005 inaugural parade in Washington, D.C.

president, vice president, their families, visiting heads of state, and other designated individuals. Secret Service special agents make travel arrangements and oversee security measures at any location that the protectee may visit.

In addition to their protective duties, Secret Service special agents have the authority to investigate certain federal crimes. They perform background investigations on any individuals or groups that might pose a threat to their protectee,

# The Department of Homeland Security

**Before** the 9/11 terrorist attacks, various matters of domestic safety and security were managed by a number of agencies overseen by several different departments. In the aftermath of the disaster, Congress began to explore the possibility of reorganizing these assorted agencies and departments under a single authority. On June 6, 2002, President George W. Bush formally proposed the formation of a new cabinet-level Department of Homeland Security. Initially, the department's primary focus was to combat terrorist threats. Since its inception, its mission has evolved to include prevention, preparedness, and response to other types of disaster as well—natural or that caused by humans. A number of different law enforcement agencies were absorbed into the new department, including the U.S. Secret Service and organizations involved in customs, immigration, and border security. The FBI, however, was not included in the reorganization.

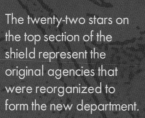

The twenty-two stars on the top section of the shield represent the original agencies that were reorganized to form the new department.

and they investigate any specific threats. Their other investigative focus reflects the fact that the U.S. Secret Service was once a branch of the U.S. Department of Treasury. Secret Service special agents investigate crimes involving money and finance, such as counterfeiting, forgery of financial certificates, and credit card fraud.

There is also a uniformed division within the U.S. Secret Service that provides security for sites such as the White House and U.S. Treasury buildings.

## DEA SPECIAL AGENT

The Drug Enforcement Administration (DEA), which is part of the Department of Justice, enforces federal laws pertaining to illicit drugs. DEA special agents investigate individuals, gangs, criminal organizations, and other groups suspected of growing, manufacturing, or distributing controlled substances. The DEA often cooperates with local, state, federal, and international law enforcement agencies during the course of their investigations. The DEA also regulates legal but dangerous drugs that are distributed for medical purposes.

A DEA special agent's primary focus is gathering information and evidence for federal cases. Special agents conduct surveillance, perform interrogations, receive tips from informants, and infiltrate drug-trafficking rings. During raids, they confiscate drugs and drug-making equipment, drug money and other assets gained through drug sales, and any other evidence necessary for a prosecution. They also spend time on paperwork, including writing reports and applying for search warrants.

In addition to special agents, there are other experts within the DEA that contribute to investigations and operations. For instance, intelligence research specialists collect, analyze, and distribute intelligence pertaining to the drug trade, such as routes, methods of smuggling, and groups involved in the manufacture of drugs. Forensic chemists analyze drugs and other evidence in the lab; they can identify properties and sometimes the likely origins of a drug.

## DEPUTY U.S. MARSHAL

The U.S. Marshals Service, which is an agency of the Department of Justice, performs law enforcement duties that are related to the federal courts and the judicial system. The Marshals Service is charged with investigating cases of escaped prisoners and other fugitives from justice. The 15 Most Wanted list highlights the most dangerous criminals on the loose in the United States. In order to apprehend fugitives, deputy U.S. marshals work cooperatively in task forces with other law enforcement agencies. They also conduct international investigations, extraditing criminals from abroad or tracking wanted fugitives from other countries suspected of being in the United States. The Marshals Service Special Operations Group can be called in to respond to crisis situations.

Deputy U.S. marshals also provide security and various services for the federal courts. They design security systems for facilities and, when necessary, guard judges, jurors, witnesses, and other figures. The U.S. Marshals Service maintains the Witness Protection Program, in which witnesses in sensitive federal cases are given new identities. Deputy U.S. marshals transport federal prisoners, serve court papers, and oversee forfeited assets. These assets can include money, property, jewelry, and other proceeds gained through drug sales or other criminal activity.

## U.S. POSTAL INSPECTOR

U.S. postal inspectors enforce more than two hundred federal laws relating to U.S. mail, the U.S. Postal Service, and postal workers. They investigate crimes related to mail, such as theft, fraud, and the mailing of illegal materials. Postal inspectors are responsible for investigating burglaries committed at post offices and assaults against mail carriers. Like any criminal investigator, a postal inspector will secure the scene, interview witnesses, and even do undercover work. The U.S. Postal Inspection

Service sometimes collaborates with other federal law enforcement agencies in cases that involve postal crimes. The agency also maintains a postal police force of officers who provide security to U.S. Postal Service facilities and property. Applicants to the U.S. Postal Inspection Service should have applicable experience or education, such as fluency in a foreign language, past employment in the U.S. Postal Service, training in accounting, computer expertise, a law degree, or law enforcement experience.

## IRS CRIMINAL INVESTIGATION SPECIAL AGENT

The Internal Revenue Service (IRS) is the arm of the Department of Treasury that collects federal taxes. Within the IRS, the Criminal Investigation (CI) unit investigates tax fraud, tax evasion, and other financial crimes. It reviews tax records and other documents related to cases of tax code violation or crimes such as money laundering. IRS Criminal Investigation special agents often cooperate in joint investigations with officials from other federal agencies, and they sometimes do undercover work.

Most of these special agents have a background in accounting or finance. They are federal law enforcement agents, however, and their training

Many crimes involve the sending of illegal documents or goods. U.S. postal inspectors handle crimes involving mail.

period includes instruction in using firearms and arresting suspects, as well as in tax law, financial investigation techniques, and cyberinvestigation.

## ATF SPECIAL AGENT

The U.S. Bureau of Alcohol, Tobacco, Firearms and Explosives (ATF) is an agency within the Department of Justice. ATF special agents enforce federal laws involving the criminal use of firearms and explosives,

A park ranger at Colorado's Mesa Verde National Park describes how the Ancestral Puebloans built the Cliff Palace and how they dealt with water shortages.

they perform arson investigations, and they investigate illegal sales of alcohol and tobacco. They oversee the regulation and licensing of firearms and explosives, and they investigate cases of illegal trafficking. The ATF enforces tax laws applying to the sales of alcohol and tobacco, and it confirms that industries are following government regulations. This reflects the origins of the bureau as a division of the IRS. ATF special agents often work with other federal law enforcement agencies, and they frequently

partner with local and state law enforcement agencies in promoting programs to fight crime and reduce violence.

## PARK RANGER AND
## U.S. PARK POLICE OFFICER

Park rangers and U.S. Park Police officers work for the National Park Service, which is an agency of the Department of the Interior. Park rangers have a huge scope of duties and responsibilities. Like any law enforcement officers, they enforce federal laws and park regulations and conduct criminal investigations, but they also serve, in a sense, as the park's ambassadors to the public. A park ranger may lead tours, organize events, give a talk on the park's geology, or instruct visitors on water safety precautions. Park rangers are responsible for the safety and security of visitors, as well as the preservation and smooth operations of the park and its resources. Many of their duties further both of these objectives—for example, park rangers manage parks, oversee campgrounds, work to prevent or control forest fires, and help in search and rescue efforts. Applicants for the position of park ranger should have a bachelor's degree in a related subject, such as science or natural resource management, or have relevant experience. This could include past work in law enforcement or a job as a park guide.

The U.S. Park Police keeps the peace and investigates crimes within the national park system. Most Park Police officers work in the Washington, D.C., area. The Park Police includes both a patrol branch and a criminal investigations branch. Job requirements are similar to those for a local police department position.

# U.S. CAPITOL POLICE

The U.S. Capitol Police is the force that ensures safety and security in the U.S. Capitol—the building in Washington, D.C., in which Congress convenes— and the surrounding complex and grounds. Policing the U.S. Capitol poses a unique challenge, since it is the workplace of U.S. senators and representatives and, at the same time, a tourist attraction open to the public. U.S. Capitol officers perform everyday law enforcement duties such as writing citations, enforcing laws, and investigating suspicious activities. The U.S. Capitol Police officers are also charged with the protection of members of Congress and their families.

# 4
# RELATED CAREERS IN LAW ENFORCEMENT

I n addition to jobs at the local, state, and federal levels, there is a wealth of opportunities in other fields that require personnel with law enforcement training and experience. Many industries and corporations, for example, hire private security guards to monitor their facilities and prevent crime. Such positions may be attractive to either former police officers or those looking for law enforcement jobs outside of police or government work.

Some of these jobs may involve general guard and patrol duty, but there are also numerous opportunities in specialized areas. Locksmithing, alarm system installation, security consultation, and other jobs involving physical security require knowledge of what makes a site vulnerable to criminal invasion. Many employment opportunities in computer security require considerable technological expertise for safeguarding information from hackers or internal security violations. Compliance inspectors scrutinize facilities to confirm that there are no violations of federal or state laws and regulations. They enforce laws pertaining to food, consumer product safety, environmental health, workplace safety, banking procedures, and much more. These positions generally require a bachelor's degree in a related field.

For job seekers interested in some aspects of police work but who do not want to become police officers, there may be openings for personnel in civilian positions—writers, photographers, statisticians, computer technicians, record keepers and so on. They may work for a police department or do consulting work when necessary. Public safety dispatchers and the experts in the forensic lab also fill essential functions for the police department.

## Security Guard

Private security firms provide services for banks, offices, factories, museums, hospitals, and other facilities. The field is expanding—concerns about security among businesses are on the rise, and some public sector jobs in areas such as prison, transportation, and municipal security are being outsourced to private firms.

The exact duties of a security guard vary depending on the particular position. Security

guards patrol and protect the premises, monitor surveillance devices such as closed circuit television (CCTV), maintain order, and enforce the employer's policies and regulations. Security guards may be expected to answer questions posed by visitors, check identification, or inspect vehicles and deliveries. They respond to any complaints or emergencies that arise, and they may have the authority to investigate

A campus safety officer at Onondaga Community College in Syracuse, New York, monitors security with the help of about 180 cameras located around the campus.

possible crimes or wrongdoings. Security guards also maintain a record of the day's incidents.

Demand for private security services is growing, and the field is becoming increasingly profession-alized and respected. States generally require that security guards be licensed and pass a background check, and some states and counties require addi-tional certification and training. Security guards

# The Military Route

**Military** service is one possible way for young people to gain experience early on for a law enforcement career. Enlistees receive general training in a number of areas—patrol, weapons training, tactics, and so on—that will give them an excellent background for police work. Military service also instills discipline and familiarizes recruits with the rank system and rules of conduct. Members of the military can often take advantage of educational programs that allow them to earn college credit during active duty.

Some service members choose to specialize in occupational fields that are directly relevant to law enforcement. The Military Police (MP), for example, patrol military bases and have jurisdiction over military personnel. Young people interested in combining military duty and higher education might consider joining the National Guard rather than one of the five branches of the military. Most local, state, and federal agencies give hiring preference to veterans of the military who have served at least three years of active duty.

Military duty equips service members with practical skills, a sense of discipline, and experience in handling crisis situations.

certified as special police officers can make arrests on the job. Although most security guards do not carry weapons, armed security guards must possess a gun license and complete any required firearms training. Previous experience in law enforcement or the military is highly desirable.

There are opportunities in private security for job seekers from every level of education. Workers with a high school diploma or GED credential can land an entry-level job if they have motivation, good interpersonal skills, and a professional appearance. A college graduate in criminal justice, with a strong background in law enforcement, may land a top position in the internal security department of a large corporation.

## Private Investigator

Private investigators are hired to carry out investigative work or provide protection. Clients turn to private investigators for a wide range of services, from surveillance work to searching through government documents. These clients may include private individuals, businesses, or organizations. Lawyers often hire private investigators to collect evidence, locate and interview witnesses, review documents, and otherwise help them in building court cases. A private investigator must be prepared to operate alone, whether in the field or, more

A private investigator performing surveillance work may photograph, videotape, or audiotape his or her subjects to document their activities.

often, behind a desk doing routine information gathering on a computer.

A private investigator may take on different types of cases, or he or she may do a particular type of work. Some private investigators specialize in areas that require previous education or experience in a certain field. They may focus on cases of arson, insurance fraud, or financial dealings. Another area of specialization is in performing background investigations. A private investigator may collect

information about an individual's personal history, such as criminal activity, employment history, credit reports, and past addresses. Companies often have background checks performed before hiring a new employee or doing business with a person or group. Individuals also have background checks done for personal reasons.

A private investigator's day may involve serving court papers, staking out a business, or photographing the scene of an accident. Individuals concerned about their safety may hire private investigators for personal protection. A husband or wife going through a divorce may hire a private investigator to conduct surveillance or investigations on his or her spouse. Private investigators often hunt for missing persons, whether they may be bail jumpers, clients' relatives, potential witnesses, or child abductors. Retail businesses hire private investigators as store detectives, mainly to prevent shoplifting and employee theft. A private investigator has to keep running progress reports on each case and may be called on to testify in court as an expert witness.

Most large private investigation agencies require previous experience, such as work in business, law, or law enforcement, and they many require a two-year or four-year degree. A private investigator must be licensed by the state. Firms look for employees who have good communication and research skills, manage time and resources efficiently, and can work well in high-pressure situations. The future job outlook for private investigators is favorable, since employment in the field is expected to rise due to increased demand for services.

## CAMPUS POLICE DEPARTMENT OFFICER

Many colleges and universities have their own police departments. The campus police department is headed by a chief of police, and the force is made up of campus police officers or campus public safety officers. Their mission is to ensure that an academic campus remains a safe and secure learning environment for students, faculty, and staff. They enforce federal, state, and local laws and uphold the school's own policies and regulations.

Campus police officers perform many of the same types of duties as local police officers on patrol do. They investigate suspicious activities, direct traffic, and respond to requests for assistance. During certain hours, especially late at night, campus police officers will provide a ride or accompany students who are nervous about walking alone. The campus police department may also organize safety and security seminars for students on topics such as crime prevention, alcohol abuse, and sexual assault.

Specific safety and security practices vary from one campus to another. On some campuses, campus police officers carry firearms; on others, they are unarmed. Many colleges and universities have installed emergency call boxes in multiple locations on school grounds. Campus police officers are notified of summons for help through a two-way radio. Like any police officer, campus police officers spend time writing up reports and, if necessary, testifying in court.

The job application, requirements, and training are similar to the hiring process for local police departments. Upon being hired, a new recruit will undergo training at a police academy before beginning on-the-job training.

## DISPATCHER

Whenever someone phones in an emergency or non-emergency request for assistance, the call goes through to a dispatcher. The dispatcher may work in a communications center within a particular police department or a central communications center operated by a city or region's public safety department. (The public safety department is composed of police, fire, and emergency services.) The dispatcher is responsible for taking information from the caller and determining the appropriate response to the situation.

The dispatcher begins with a set of standard questions. If the situation is not an emergency, then the caller is transferred or directed to the appropriate authorities. As the dispatcher learns more details, he or she prioritizes the incident. For example, a recent theft in which the suspect had just left the premises would take priority over a break-in that had happened earlier in the week and only recently been discovered. The dispatcher decides which emergency personnel should be sent to the scene and locates the unit that is closest to the emergency. He or she relays the information to

A dispatch supervisor for the Morgan County Sheriff's Department in Jacksonville, Illinois, records information after receiving a 911 call.

the appropriate unit by radio or computer. The dispatcher then monitors the unit for possible further requests. Throughout the process, the dispatcher enters all pertinent information into a computer record.

Strong communication skills and the ability to function well under pressure are essential for dispatchers. A dispatcher must be ready to deal with a range of crises and difficult circumstances, whether they may be a call from a panicked crime victim or from a young child with an injured parent. After being hired, recruits undergo a training program intended to prepare them for any situation.

## FORENSIC TECHNICIAN AND FORENSIC SCIENTIST

Forensic science is the application of scientific methods to the field of law. Forensic scientists and technicians help investigate crimes by studying the physical evidence that might yield clues about how a crime occurred or who committed the crime. The field of forensics brings together a broad range of sciences and areas of specialization. These include disciplines that are relevant for obvious reasons, such as medicine, odontology (the study of teeth), entomology (the study of insects), physics, biology, and chemistry. More surprisingly, there are forensic applications of anthropology, psychology, accounting, engineering, art, linguistics, mathematics, seismology, and other areas. These are just a few of the fields that are related to forensics.

A single crime scene can yield evidence pertinent to a variety of forensic disciplines. There may be fingerprints, pools and spatters of blood, footprints, bullet fragments, pertinent documents, insects, and trace evidence such as hairs or glass chips.

Forensic technicians and forensic scientists work in particular areas of investigation. Crime scene technicians collect, label, and preserve evidence from the scene of the crime for later examination and analysis in a laboratory. They take precautions to avoid contaminating the scene or any piece of evidence. Forensic chemists and trace evidence examiners perform lab tests on evidence of all kinds—stained clothing, unidentified substances, fibers, suspected drugs, body fluids, and much more—in order to learn more information about the crime. Latent print examiners analyze fingerprints, palm prints, and footprints from the crime scene and identify suspects by matching the evidence to their known prints. Medical examiners perform autopsies on bodies and present conclusions on the circumstances of death. Toxicologists analyze blood and other body fluids for the presence of drugs, alcohol, or poisons.

Firearm and toolmark examiners determine whether specific firearms or tools, such as

screwdrivers or hammers, were used during a crime. Every firearm leaves unique markings on the bullet, and every tool leaves a distinctive mark as well. Firearm experts may be required to examine gunpowder residue patterns or give an opinion on a bullet's trajectory. Questioned document

A New York State Police forensic investigator photographs a possible exit site of a bullet.

examiners also determine whether documents are forgeries, and they analyze paper, ink, and writing instruments for possible evidence.

Education, experience, and licensing requirements for forensic technicians and forensic scientists vary greatly depending on the exact position. Entry-level technicians should have a high school diploma or a GED credential, and they should have relevant education or training in their area. Forensic scientists generally have an advanced degree and are considered experts in their fields.

## POLYGRAPH EXAMINERS

Polygraph examiners administer polygraph—lie detector—tests, asking the subject a series of questions while the machine records physical responses. The polygraph attachments measure respiration, heart rate, blood pressure, and electrical resistance of the skin, which is affected by sweating. Results are recorded on rolls of paper or displayed on a computer screen.

Before formulating the questions, the examiner reviews the details of the case. The questions must be very clearly worded and have a yes or no answer. Later, the examiner analyzes the charts of the physical responses and concludes whether or not the subject was being truthful or deceptive, or if the results are inconclusive.

# THE FUTURE OF LAW ENFORCEMENT

The job outlook in law enforcement is favorable for qualified candidates. Employment is expected to increase, according to the U.S. Department of Labor's Bureau of Labor Statistics. This increase is partly due to normal population growth. In addition, after the terrorist attacks of 9/11, American society became more fixated on security concerns. There is expected to be more competition for state and federal positions than for jobs in local police departments.

Law enforcement departments encourage minority and women candidates to apply, with the goal of building a force that reflects the diversity of the communities they serve. Nonetheless, minorities and women are still underrepresented in the field, especially at the state and local levels.

What skills and abilities should we expect of tomorrow's officers and agents? They will be technologically adept, familiar with cutting-edge crime-fighting tools as well as with methods of

foiling high-tech crimes. There will be more specialists focusing on particular aspects of law enforcement. They will be more highly educated. Officers will continue to become more involved with their communities, working hand in hand with citizens and community leaders, rather than trying to impose order. Law enforcement organizations will continue to take measures to prevent terrorism and to prepare for possible attacks, from federal agencies dealing in intelligence down to local police

New recruits are welcomed to the Cleveland Police Department. Many cities in Ohio and across the nation make an effort to recruit minority officers into police forces.

departments that would deploy the first responders to the scene. In addition, as law enforcement missions evolve, there will be innovative approaches introduced to prevent and combat crime.

## TECHNOLOGICAL ADVANCES

The modern law enforcement officer is expected to be computer literate, and the level of technology used in the field will continue to increase. Databases

# Law Enforcement in "Indian Country"

**The** U.S. government recognizes Native American tribes as "dependent domestic nations" entitled to tribal sovereignty and self-determination. This means that they have their own tribal governments, courts, and law enforcement agencies. According to the U.S. Department of Justice, tribal law enforcement agencies keep the peace in a total area of more than 55,000,000 acres (22,258,000 hectares)—that's about the size of the state of Minnesota. Much of this territory lies in geographically isolated areas. This presents challenges for law enforcement agencies, especially when there are limited personnel and resources.

Investigations on tribal land, referred to as "Indian country" in the legal system, can involve federal, state, and tribal law enforcement agencies. The FBI or other federal agencies have jurisdiction over felonies and some misdemeanors. Jurisdiction also depends on where the crime was committed and whether the offender and victim of a crime were Native American or non–Native American. Cases often require that multiple law enforcement agencies cooperate in the investigation.

and networks are important tools in investigating crimes. The National Crime Information Center (NCIC), for example, contains information on missing persons, stolen goods, and criminal histories. The National Incident-Based Reporting System (NIBRS), a system managed by the FBI, contains detailed data on crime incidents. These databases and many others are constantly being updated and refined. Officers can access some databases through mobile data terminals in police vehicles.

In addition, many larger police departments use crime-mapping analysis to fight crime more effectively. The geographical locations of incidents are plotted on a digitized map. Departments can identify areas with high rates of offenses or calls for help, and they can use this information when planning strategies for preventing and targeting crime.

Even as crime-fighting tools are becoming more high tech, criminals are using more cutting-edge techniques. A computer user can commit fraud, burglary, or sabotage without ever leaving the desk. The criminal can use a computer to target underage children or stalk a victim. In addition, criminals sometimes illegally access or exploit networks containing personal or sensitive information. As criminals have grown more technologically savvy, there has been an increase in some types of economic crimes, such as theft of

intellectual property, various types of fraud, and identity theft. Computer and economic crime investigations can easily cross state or national boundaries. Law enforcement officers on every level are becoming more adept in investigating and combating computer crimes, from specialized units in some police departments and federal agencies, down to the patrol officer who reports to the scene.

Internet crime-mapping, using maps such as this one of Oakland, California (http://www.crimemapping.com), can help police officers identify crime trends and develop crime fighting strategies for a specific area.

Technological advances have also supplied police with updated weaponry, from high-powered firearms to nonlethal alternatives. In the future, an officer may stop a suspect by immobilizing him or her in a net of sticky foam. Nonlethal weapons can be controversial, though. The Taser, a device that delivers an electric shock of fifty thousand volts, has been criticized due to cases in which the subjects have died.

# CCTV

**Closed** circuit television (CCTV) is a valuable and controversial safety and surveillance measure. Security cameras transmit a signal that is picked up only by specific receivers, and the video is displayed on a monitor. CCTV is common in many public places and workplaces. Many police departments have CCTV cameras installed at traffic intersections or high-crime locations.

Around central London, the CCTV surveillance blanket is so complete that the area is known as the "Ring of Steel." New York City has begun installing a similar system in lower Manhattan, the first such large-scale network linked to a single surveillance center in the United States. The technology is capable of identifying unattended packages and reading license plates on cars. Cameras can function in the dark and rotate to track moving objects.

Proponents of CCTV surveillance claim that it could deter criminals, especially terrorists, and serve as a valuable tool in identifying suspects. Critics argue that CCTV violates citizens' privacy and does not reduce crime.

CCTV cameras mounted outdoors are becoming an increasingly common sight in many large cities.

## ISSUES IN POLICING

The law enforcement system in the United States is not perfect. Police officers face personal and institutional challenges as part of the job, and the media regularly reports on accounts of police misconduct. Police departments are constantly considering new reforms, policies, and approaches to law enforcement that will improve safety for officers and citizens alike.

Even under ideal circumstances, police officers will have to combat high crime rates in urban areas. On occasion, they will have to go into potentially life-threatening situations, and they will hear of colleagues who were injured or killed in the line of duty. Departments sometimes need to adjust to funding cuts, even as their duties and costs increase. The stress of the job can take a toll on officers, in both their professional and personal lives.

Incidents of police misconduct further add to the challenges facing police departments. Such incidents include the use of excessive force, corruption, sexual abuse, and discrimination on the basis of race, sex, religion, disability, or other factors. In addition to the miscarriage of justice and the injury done to the victims of police misconduct, these incidents can damage the public image of the police force and erode the community's trust in its officers. There

Police officers on motorcycles escort the funeral procession for Philadelphia police officer Chuck Cassidy, who was shot and killed in the line of duty. Death is an ongoing risk for law enforcement officers.

has been much debate on the roots of police misconduct and the best means of prevention. Many experts agree that departments tend to have deficient accountability systems and need to improve their internal investigation practices. Other recommendations include dealing with officers with a history of misconduct, improving recruitment and training standards, and increasing community engagement.

## COMMUNITY POLICING

Community policing is one example of an innovative strategy that has been a success. Since the 1980s, many police departments have adopted a community policing (also called community-oriented policing, or COP) approach to controlling crime and disorder. This philosophy of policing holds that police officers should not distance themselves from the public. Community policing officers share information, build trust, and work in partnership with private citizens. In addition to fighting crime, they cooperate with the community to implement prevention and problem-solving strategies.

Community policing programs seek to address the root causes of crime, taking steps to raise the overall quality of life for residents, as well as improving public safety and reducing fear of crime. Community policing officers try to establish ties to

governments, residents, schools, hospitals, businesses, social welfare organizations, and other institutions in the areas they patrol. Community members are encouraged to share their concerns and priorities, and officers explain their goals and tactics for confronting crime and disorder. They attend community events and hold meetings and forums for concerned citizens. In some cases, they may serve as mediators when there is disagreement

A North Miami Beach police officer on bike patrol shakes hands with a neighborhood store owner. Community policing strategies encourage engagement with community members.

on the best approach toward tackling a problem in the community. Community policing officers may also work with outside agencies and law enforcement departments in developing programs and services for the community.

Some critics have dismissed the community policing model as a fad and resisted its implementation. Nonetheless, the strategy has proven effective in many areas and will likely continue to expand.

# GLOSSARY

**agency** A division or office of the government.

**arson** The crime of intentionally setting fire to a building or other property.

**bailiff** An officer of a court of law entrusted with duties such as keeping order in the courtroom and executing writs and processes.

**beat** In law enforcement, an officer's assigned area of patrol.

**bribery** The act or practice of giving someone money or favors in order to influence that person's actions or judgment.

**citation** An official summons, especially to appear in court, or an official notice of a charge of a petty offense.

**curriculum** The courses of study offered by an educational institution.

**customs** The inspection of goods and baggage entering a country.

**deploy** To position systematically or strategically.

**felony** A serious crime; specifically, a federal crime for which the punishment may be death or imprisonment for more than a year.

first responder  The law enforcement officer or other personnel who arrives first at the scene of an accident or disaster.

intelligence  Secret information, especially about an enemy or potential enemy; also, the agency or unit responsible for gathering and distributing such information.

morale  The emotional and mental conditions of a person or group regarding qualities such as confidence, cheerfulness, and courage.

parole  The conditional release of a prisoner before the end of the maximum prison sentence.

personnel  The people employed at an organization or place of work.

probation  The trial process or period in which a person's fitness for employment at a certain job is tested; also, the act of suspending an offender's sentence and allowing him or her to go free subject to certain conditions.

surveillance  Close observation or monitoring, often of a person or group under suspicion.

testify  To state or declare under oath, usually in a court of law.

# FOR MORE INFORMATION

American Criminal Justice Association
Lambda Alpha Epsilon
P.O. Box 601047
Sacramento, CA 95860
(916) 484-6553
Web site: http://www.acjalae.org
This is an organization of students and professionals in the field of criminal justice.

*American Police Beat*
43 Thorndike St., 2nd Floor
Cambridge, MA 02141
(800) 234-0056
Web site: http://www.apbweb.com
This magazine and Web site address issues in the personal and professional lives of law enforcement officers.

Canadian Police Association
141 Catherine Street, Suite 100
Ottawa, ON K2P 1C3
Canada

(613) 231-4168
Web site: http://www.cpa-acp.ca
This is an organization of police personnel in Canada.

*FBI Law Enforcement Bulletin*
Federal Bureau of Investigation
935 Pennsylvania Avenue NW
Washington, DC 20535
Web site: http://www.fbi.gov/publications/leb/leb.htm
This monthly publication highlights current issues of
interest and concern to the law enforcement
community.

**International Association of Chiefs of Police (IAC)**
515 N. Washington Street
Alexandria, VA 22314
(703) 836-6767
Web site: http://www.theiacp.org
The IAC is dedicated to providing global leadership in
policing.

**International Association of Women Police**
P.O. Box 184
Marble Hill, GA 30148
Web site: http://www.iawp.org
This organization formed with a mission to strengthen,
unite, and raise the profile of women in criminal justice
internationally.

**Royal Canadian Mounted Police**
RCMP Public Affairs and Communications Services
Headquarters Building
1200 Vanier Parkway
Ottawa, ON K1A 0R2
Canada
(613) 993-7267
Web site: http://www.rcmp-grc.gc.ca
The Royal Canadian Mounted Police, or Mounties, is
Canada's national police service.

**USAJOBS**
(703) 724-1850
Web site: http://www.usajobs.gov
This is the official job site of the federal government.

# WEB SITES

Due to the changing nature of Internet links,
Rosen Publishing has developed an online list of
Web sites related to the subject of this book. This
site is updated regularly. Please use this link to
access the list:

http://www.rosenlinks.com/ccj/lawe

# FOR FURTHER READING

Ackerman, Thomas H. *FBI Careers: The Ultimate Guide to Landing a Job as One of America's Finest*. 2nd ed. Indianapolis, IN: JIST Works, 2005.

Ackerman, Thomas H. *Federal Law Enforcement Careers: Profiles of 250 High-Powered Positions and Surefire Tactics for Getting Hired*. 2nd ed. Indianapolis, IN: JIST Works, 2006.

Baden, Michael. *Dead Reckoning: The New Science of Catching Killers*. New York, NY: Simon & Schuster, 2001.

Harr, J. Scott, and Karen M. Hess. *Careers in Criminal Justice and Related Fields: From Internship to Promotion*. 5th ed. Belmont, CA: Wadsworth Publishing, 2006.

Harris, Elizabeth Snoke. *Crime Scene Science Fair Projects*. New York, NY: Lark Books, 2006.

Henderson, Harry. *Career Opportunities in Computers and Cyberspace*. New York, NY: Checkmark Books/Facts On File, 2004.

Reeves, Diane Lindsey, and Don Rauf. *Career Ideas for Teens in Government and Public Service*. New York, NY: Facts On File, 2005.

Reeves, Diane Lindsey, and Gail Karlitz. *Career Ideas for Teens in Law and Public Safety.* New York, NY: Checkmark Books, 2006.

Schroeder, Donald J. *Barron's How to Prepare for the Police Officer Examination.* 7th ed. Hauppauge, NY: Barron's Educational Series, 2005.

Taylor, Dorothy L. *Jumpstarting Your Career: An Internship Guide for Criminal Justice.* 2nd ed. Upper Saddle River, NJ: Prentice Hall, 2004.

# BIBLIOGRAPHY

Axelrod, Alan, and Guy Antinozzi. *The Complete Idiot's Guide to Criminal Investigation.* Indianapolis, IN: Pearson Education, Inc., 2003.

California Commission on Peace Officer Standards & Training. "Regular Basic Course." 2008. Retrieved September 12, 2008 (http://www.post.ca.gov/training/bt_bureau/regular.asp).

Douglas, John E. *John Douglas's Guide to Landing a Career in Law Enforcement.* New York, NY: McGraw-Hill, 2005.

Echaore-McDavid, Susan. *Career Opportunities in Law Enforcement, Security, and Protective Services.* 2nd ed. New York, NY: Checkmark Books, 2006.

Koletar, Joseph W. *The FBI Career Guide: Inside Information on Getting Chosen for and Succeeding in One of the Toughest, Most Prestigious Jobs in the World.* New York, NY: AMACOM, 2006.

Lambert, Stephen, and Debra Regan. *Great Jobs for Criminal Justice Majors.* 2nd ed. New York, NY: McGraw Hill, 2007.

Los Angeles Police Department. "William J. Bratton, Chief of Police." 2004–2008. Retrieved September 12, 2008 (http://www.lapdonline.org/lapd_command_staff/comm_bio_view/7574).

Ortmeier, P. J. *Introduction to Law Enforcement and Criminal Justice*. 2nd ed. Upper Saddle River, NJ: Pearson Education, Inc., 2006.

Stinchcomb, James. *Opportunities in Law Enforcement and Criminal Justice Careers*. Chicago, IL: VGM Career Books, 2003.

Texas Department of Public Safety. "Texas Rangers." 2000. Retrieved September 12, 2008 (http://www.txdps.state.tx.us/director_staff/texas_rangers).

U.S. Bureau of Labor Statistics. "Occupational Outlook Handbook, 2008–2009 Edition: Police and Detectives." 2007. Retrieved September 12, 2008 (http://www.bls.gov/oco/ocos160.htm).

Wilson, Jeremy M. *Community Policing in America*. New York, NY: Routledge, 2006.

# INDEX

## ABOUT THE AUTHOR

Corona Brezina has written over a dozen titles for Rosen Publishing. Several of her previous books have also focused on career possibilities for young adults, such as *Careers in Forensics: Careers as a Medical Examiner*. She lives in Chicago.

## PHOTO CREDITS

Cover, pp. 1, 3, 7, 25, 47, 70, 87 © www.istockphoto.com/ GBlackeley, © www.istockphoto.com/wh1600, © www. istockphoto.com/tobkatrina, © www.istockphoto.com/ stevedangers, © www.istockphoto.com/jcarillet; p. 5 Charles Ommanney/Getty Images; pp. 9, 17, 22–23, 57, 88–89 © AP Images; pp. 12–13 © Joe Sohm/The ImageWorks; pp. 28–29 Stephen Chernin/Getty Images; p. 31 Scott Alfieri/Getty Images; p. 34 © Mitch Wojnarowicz/Amsterdam Recorder/The Image Works; pp. 38–39, 98–99 © Jeff Greenberg/The Image Works; pp. 42, 76–77 © Bob Daemmrich/The Image Works; p. 45 © Monika Graff/The Image Works; pp. 50–51, 54–55 © Rob Crandall/The Image Works; p. 52 Library of Congress Prints and Photographs Division; p. 59 Matthew Cavanaugh/ Getty Images; p. 65 Jeff Swensen/Getty Images; pp. 66–67 © Teake Zuidema/The Image Works; pp. 72–73 © Syracuse Newspapers/G. Wright/The Image Works; p. 74 Photo Courtesy of U.S. Army; p. 81 © Journal-Courier/Kendra Helmer/The Images Works; pp. 84–85 © Syracuse Newspapers/D. Nett/The Image Works; p. 94 Shutterstock.com; p. 96 William Thomas Cain/Getty Images.

Designer: Les Kanturek; Editor: Nicholas Croce
Photo Researcher: Amy Feinberg

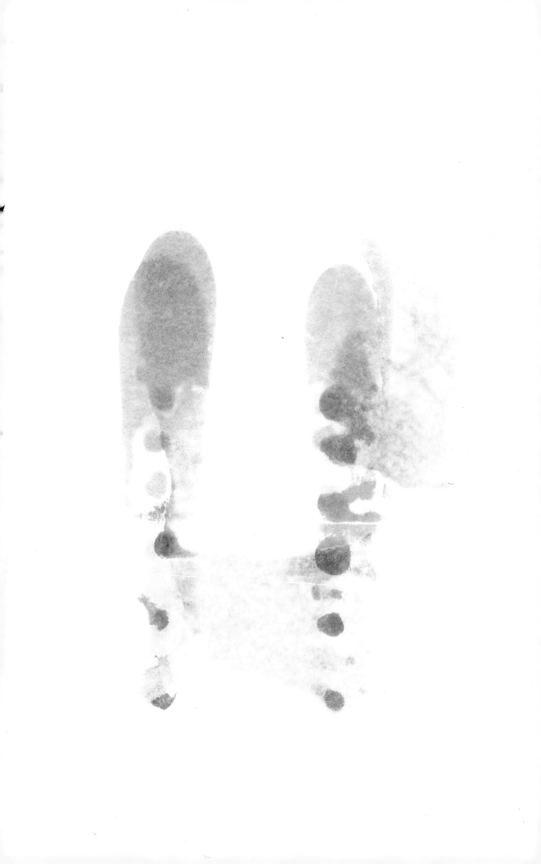

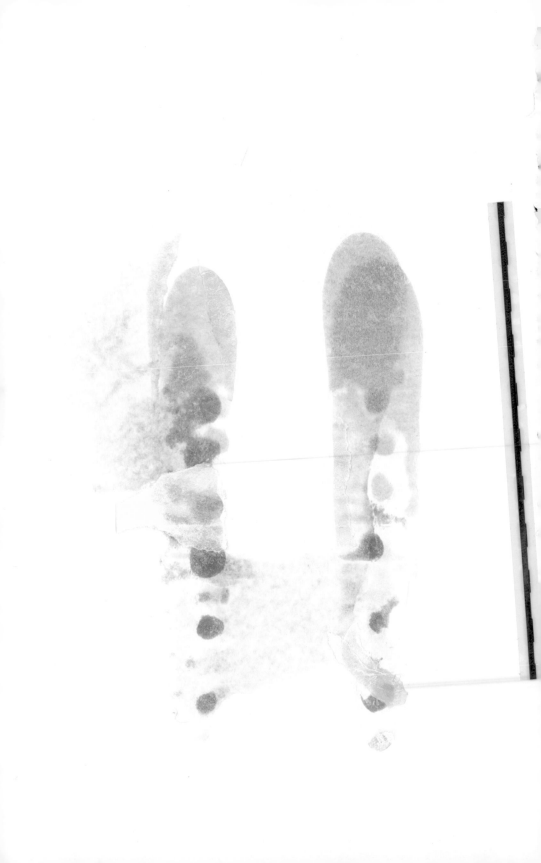